Moma
Christ

THE LEPRECHAUN
LIBRARY

Avril Rodway
Illustrated by Mark Reddy

HUTCHINSON
London Melbourne Sydney Auckland Johannesburg

Lavender has been a favourite bath herb for hundreds of years, as well as a popular fragrance for soap. According to tradition, Mary washed Jesus's swaddling clothes with lavender, and it has maintained its association with laundering ever since. Lavender sachets are still made to place among clothes: the sweet scent not only perfumes the clothes, but keeps moths away as well. Lavender water is used to soothe headaches and is said to relieve toothache. If clippings from lavender bushes are burned on an open fire, they will scent the room – a wonderful autumnal smell. Like rose petals, lavender flowers are a traditional ingredient of pot-pourri.

I had often occasion to notice the use that was made of fragments and small opportunities in Cranford; the rose-leaves that were gathered ere they fell to make into a pot-pourri for some one who had no garden; the little bundles of lavender flowers sent to strew the drawers of some town-dweller, or to burn in the chamber of some invalid. Things that many would despise, and notions which it seemed scarcely worth while to perform, were all attended to in Cranford.

MRS GASKELL: CRANFORD

Lavender

The legend of how the bay tree came into being is, perhaps, the most famous of all the stories of nymphs and mortals being changed into other shapes to escape the attentions of the gods. Daphne, the daughter of the river god Peneus, had vowed to spend her life in perpetual virginity; when Apollo, the god of poetry, pursued her she prayed for deliverance. Her prayers were answered and, as he clasped her, she turned into a bay tree in his arms. (The fifteenth-century artist Del Pollaiuolo depicted this scene in a beautiful and famous painting.) Apollo was heartbroken, and thereafter made his wreath of bay leaves instead of the oak leaves he had formerly worn.

Bay was used thereafter to crown victorious athletes and soldiers, and great poets, as a sign of their pre-eminence. Many poets in all ages mention the coveted bay tree in their poems – but they often call it laurel or laurels from its botanical name *Laurus nobilis*. Indeed, the bay laurel is sometimes confused with the cherry laurel (*Prunus laurocerasus)*, but this is poisonous and must never be used in cooking. Nicholas Culpeper has a great deal to say about the medicinal virtues of bay, and maintains that it 'resisteth witchcraft very potently, as also all the evils old Saturn can do the body of man, and they are not a few . . . neither witch nor devil, thunder nor lightning, will hurt a man where a bay tree is.'

The seventeenth-century poet Andrew Marvell summed up the story of bay most beautifully in his poem 'The Garden':

> The Gods, that mortal beauty chase,
> Still in a tree did end their race.
> Apollo hunted Daphne so,
> Only that she might laurel grow.
> And Pan did after Syrinx speed,
> Not as a nymph, but for a reed.

Bay

The hawthorn has long been used by country folk: the young buds in salads as 'bread and cheese', the flowers, dried, in pot-pourri and the berries, cooked with apples, to make jelly. In Norfolk, according to the Folk Lore Society, 'It was an old custom, in most farmhouses, for any servant who could bring in a branch of hawthorn in full bloom, on the 1st May, to be entitled to receive a dish of cream for breakfast.'

The flowers of the field
Have a sweet smell:
Meadowsweet, tansy, thyme,
And faint-hearted pimpernel;
But sweeter even than these,
The silver of the may
Wreathed is with incense for
The Judgment Day.

An apple, a child, dust,
When falls the evening rain,
Wild brier's spicèd leaves,
Breathe memories again;
With further memory fraught,
The silver of the may
Wreathed is with incense for
The Judgment Day.

WALTER DE LA MARE: 'THE HAWTHORN HATH A DEATHLY SMELL' (EXTRACT)

Hawthorn

Traditionally the herb of friendship and remembrance, rosemary once played a part in both wedding ceremonies and funerals. An early nineteenth-century herbal contains the following information:

The ancients were well acquainted with this shrub, which has always been supposed to strengthen the memory. Hence the frequent allusions to it in our poets; as in Shakespeare, 'There's rosemary, that's for remembrance.' On this account it became the emblem of fidelity in lovers, and was worn at weddings; and probably for the same reason at funerals, at which, in some parts of England, it is still distributed among the company, who frequently throw the sprigs into the grave along with the corpse.

Its name comes from Latin and means 'foam of the sea', or 'sea dew'; as Venus, the goddess of love, arose from the sea, rosemary also had amatory associations. Samuel Butler writes:

> The sea his mother Venus came on;
> And hence some rev'rend men approve
> of rosemary in making love.

There are a number of charming legends associated with rosemary. One is that its flowers were white until the Virgin Mary threw her blue cloak over the plant to dry, when the flowers turned the same colour and have remained so to this day. It is also said that rosemary will never grow taller than the height of Christ when he was on earth.

Rosemary may be used in cooking – it is particularly good with lamb and chicken. It can also be made into a hair rinse, and some herbalists use it to treat baldness. The pretty little blue flowers are very attractive to bees.

Rosemary

Dill has always had the reputation of being able to put witches to flight – and it was also popular as an ingredient in love potions. Its name comes from *dilla*, an Icelandic word meaning 'lull', and dill water made from the herb has been used for many years as a soothing potion and to promote good digestion. In cooking, the dried leaves sold as 'dill weed' add flavour to sauces, fish and egg dishes, and the seeds to pickles, soups and salads.

Canny moment, lucky fit;
Is the lady lighter yet?
Be it lad or be it lass,
Sign wi' cross, and sain wi' mass.

Trefoil, vervain, John's wort, dill,
Hinders witches of their will;
Weel is them, that weel may
Fast upon Saint Andrew's day.

Saint Bride and her brat,
Saint Colme and his cat,
Saint Michael and his spear,
Keep the house frae reif and wear.

SIR WALTER SCOTT: 'THE NATIVITY CHANT'

Dill

This delightful sweet herb was brought to this country by the Romans and was much used by them and the Greeks. Bees love it, and Greek honey, gathered from wild thyme, is prized throughout the world for its marvellous flavour. It has antiseptic qualities, and was used in the old days for fumigating and for embalming bodies. The ordinary garden thyme and the lemon thyme are most used in cooking, and thyme is one of the ingredients of bouquets garnis. It was mentioned in a seventeenth-century recipe for conjuring up fairies, with whom thyme was traditionally associated: 'put into the glasse . . . the flowers or toppes of wild thyme . . . and the thyme must be gathered neare the side of a hill where fairies used to be.'

In my garden grew plenty of thyme,
It would flourish by night and by day.
O'er the wall came a lad, he took all that I had
And stole my thyme away.

O! And I was a damsel so fair,
But fairer I wished to appear,
So I washed me in milk, and I dressed me in silk,
And put the sweet thyme in my hair.

'DEVONSHIRE SONG'

Thyme

In whatever country catmint – or catnip – is found, its name signifies that cats love it. It is called *cataire herbe aux chats* in France, *gattaria* in Italy, *Katzonnepte* in Germany, and so on. Conversely, rats are said to hate it. It is reputed to be very calming to the stomach and to be an effective mild sedative.

The whole of this plant has a strong scent between Mint and Pennyroyal. It is called Catmint, because cats are very fond of it, especially when it is withered, when they will roll themselves on it, tear it to pieces and chew it with great pleasure. Ray observes, that plants which he transplanted from the fields into his garden were always destroyed by the cats, unless he protected them with thorns till they had taken good root and come into flower; but that they never meddled with the plants raised from seed. Hence the old saying,

> If you set it, the cats will eat it;
> If you sow it, the cats don't know it.

THOMAS GREEN: THE UNIVERSAL HERBAL

Catmint

Fennel is a beautiful plant, closely related to dill. But the two should not be planted close together or they will cross-fertilize. Fennel seeds are often used in cooking, being particularly good in fish dishes. Medicinally, fennel was once considered an aid to slimming, and a cure for sore eyes. Pliny lists twenty-two remedies which include fennel – no bad record for any plant. It was also used in witchcraft, and is mentioned in the eleventh-century Nine-Herbs Charm:

> Thyme and Fennel, a pair great in power,
> The Wise Lord, holy in heaven,
> Wrought these herbs while He hung on the cross;
> He placed and put them in the seven worlds to
> aid all, poor and rich.

This incantation mentions nine plants, each of which was used to heal a different illness. When one of the plants was to be used, the herbalist would intone the correct part of the verse over it.

> Be careful, ere ye enter in, to fill
> Your baskets high
> With fennel green, and balm, and golden pines,
> Savory, latter-mint, and columbines,
> Cool parsley, basil sweet and sunny thyme;
> Yes, every flower and leaf of every clime,
> All gather'd in the dewy morning.

JOHN KEATS: 'ENDYMION'

Fennel

The rowan or mountain ash has long been regarded as a power against witches. As the Folk Lore Society tells us: 'May 2 is the Eve of the Invention of the Cross and is associated with the popular belief that branches and twigs collected on this day from the mountain ash, rowan or witchen tree are protective against the evil influences of witches and others.' Traditionally, two twigs should be bound together in the form of a cross with red thread or wool, and the amulet worn or otherwise displayed. The Denham Tracts of 1895 bear this out: 'I have seen a twig or rowan tree wound round with dozens of yards of "reed thread", i.e. red thread, placed visibly in the window, as a protection against the influence of witches and boggleboes.' In *Puck of Pook's Hill*, by Rudyard Kipling, Puck mentioned the fact that he does not mind rowan as proof of his goodness.

'By Oak, Ash and Thorn,' cried Puck, taking off his cap, 'I like you too. Sprinkle a plenty salt on the biscuit, Dan, and I'll eat it with you. That'll show you the sort of person I am. Some of us' – he went on, with his mouth full – 'couldn't abide Salt, or Horse-shoes over a door, or Mountain-ash berries, or Running Water, or Cold Iron, or the sound of Church Bells. But I'm Puck!'

Rowan

The mandrake, one of the most feared plants in herbal lore, signifies 'horror' in the language of flowers. Thomas Newton in his *Herball to the Bible* wrote: 'It is supposed to be a creature having life, engendered under the earth of the seed of some dead person put to death for murder.' This rather sordid legend is, no doubt, one reason why it was universally regarded with awe and terror.

The root was held to look like the human form, either male or female, though Nicholas Culpeper remarks disparagingly that 'it really resembles a carrot or parsnip.'

Mandrake is a powerful narcotic and was much used as a painkiller and to produce insensibility during operations, and it had a high reputation as an aphrodisiac. The root (with perhaps a little helpful additional carving) was often dried and sold as an amulet or fertility charm in the Middle Ages, and various superstitions were associated with the gathering of the plant. These were probably fostered by the herb-vendors, who wanted to keep the price high and, accordingly, to discourage people from gathering it for themselves. Legend had it that the mandrake shrieked when pulled from the ground – and that those who heard this shriek would die. This account of how to obtain the root comes from a twelfth-century bestiary:

The man who is to gather it must fly round about it; must take great care that he does not touch it; then let him take a dog – let it be tied to it – which has been close tied up, and has fasted 3 days – let it be shown bread, and called from afar; the dog will draw it to him; the root will break; it will send forth a cry; the dog will fall down dead at the cry which he will hear – such virtue this herb has, that none can hear of it, but he must always die. When one has this root, it is of great value for medicine, for it cures of every infirmity – except only death.

Mandrake

This sinister but beautiful herb is very poisonous (avoid touching it if you find it). The berries, black and shining, and the purple-coloured flowers make the plant very attractive. Deadly nightshade was an ingredient in the traditional witches' ointment: it produced hallucinogenic effects such as the sensation of flying. The drug belladonna is extracted from this plant; its anaesthetic properties – it numbs the skin and induces sleep – have given rise to another description of the plant, 'sleep-bearing solanum'.

'Wednesday 11th of July. Saw the Deadly Nightshade –
Atropa Belladonna.'

I was alone, exploring some derelict outhouses. I suddenly came upon the plant. It looked the picture of evil and also the picture of health. . . . I knew that every part of it was poisonous, I knew too that it was beautiful. . . . I stood on the threshold, not daring to go in, staring at the button-bright berries and the dull, purplish, hairy, bell-shaped flowers reaching out towards me. I felt that the plant could poison me, even if I didn't touch it, and that if I didn't eat it, it would eat me, it looked so hungry, in spite of all the nourishment it was getting.

L. P. HARTLEY: THE GO-BETWEEN

Deadly Nightshade

Legends surrounding the elder tree are confusing in the extreme. One maintains that Christ was crucified on a cross made of elder, another that Judas Iscariot hanged himself on an elder tree. In some traditions, elder is regarded as holy wood and is therefore never struck by lightning; witches fear it for the same reason. Other traditions claim that it is liked by witches. However, gipsies maintain that it is a plant wholly beneficial to man, and they will never burn it. If you pick the flowers to make wine, the berries to make jam or syrup and the buds to eat, you should always tell the tree what you are doing, so magical are its properties.

Nearer home, beside the brook, was an old elder tree which was said to bleed human blood when cut, and that was because it was no ordinary tree, but a witch. Men and boys of a former generation had caught her listening outside the window of a neighbour's cottage and chased her with pitchforks until she reached a brook. Then, being a witch, she could not cross running water, so had turned herself into an elder tree on the bank . . . Edmund and Laura once took a table knife, intending to cut it, but their courage failed them. 'What if it should really bleed? And what if the witch came out of it and ran after us?'

FLORA THOMPSON: LARK RISE TO CANDLEFORD

Elder

All parts of the dandelion have been useful to mankind for many years, from the roots, which can be made into a coffee substitute, to the leaves, which are delicious in salads. Medically the plant has diuretic properties, which accounts for its old name of 'piss-a-bed'. Dandelion wine, made from the flowers, is one for the connoisseur; Mrs Beeton's old recipe for it is given below:

Ingredients. – 4 quarts of dandelion flowers, 4 quarts of boiling water, 3 lbs. of loaf sugar, 1 inch whole ginger, 1 lemon, the thinly-pared rind of 1 orange, 1 tablespoonful of brewer's yeast or $\frac{1}{4}$ oz. of compressed yeast moistened with water.

Method. – Put the petals of the flowers into a bowl, pour over them the boiling water, let the bowl remain covered for 3 days, meanwhile stirring it well and frequently. Strain the liquid into a preserving pan, add the rinds of the orange and lemon, both of which should be pared off in thin fine strips, the sugar, ginger, and the lemon previously stripped of its white pith and thinly sliced. Boil gently for about $\frac{1}{2}$ an hour, and when cool add the yeast spread on a piece of toast. Allow it to stand for 2 days, then turn it into a cask, keep it well bunged down for 8 or 9 weeks, and bottle the wine for use.

MRS BEETON: BOOK OF HOUSEHOLD MANAGEMENT (1907 EDITION)

Dandelion

Another name for garlic, rather surprisingly, is 'poor man's treacle'. It has always had a reputation for being effective against powers of evil, from the time when the Greeks placed it at crossroads as an offering to Hecate, goddess of witchcraft, and Ulysses escaped from Circe's spells thanks partly to its help. Hated by vampires, garlic has long been considered a powerful deterrent to them. According to Muslim legend, when the Devil left the Garden of Eden garlic sprang from the place where his left foot trod, and onion from under his right foot. Garlic has strong antiseptic and germicidal properties and is of course invaluable in cookery:

At last she told me something that I did not know – about garlic . . . As do – as *must* – all good cooks, she used quantities of that bulb. It occurred to me at once that this was London and her work was social. Garlic is all very well on the bridge between Beaucaire and Tarascon. . . . But in an *atelier de couture* in the neighbourhood of Hanover Square! . . . The lady answered mysteriously: No: there is no objection if only you take enough and train your organs to the assimilation. The perfume of allium officinale attends only on those timorous creatures who have not the courage as it were to wallow in that vegetable.

FORD MADOX FORD: PROVENCE

Garlic

Wormwood, or 'old woman', has many literary associations. Its botanical name *Artemisia* is said to have arisen because the goddess Artemis gave the herb to Chiron the centaur to use in his work of healing, and he named it after her. Another legend is that it sprang up in the slime left by the 'worm' or serpent when it was driven out of the Garden of Eden. It is not used in cooking, but is one of the ingredients of absinthe and vermouth. Medicinally, it was regarded as an antidote to drunkenness, as a tonic, stimulant, febrifuge and destroyer of worms. Wormwood is mentioned twelve times in the Bible, from which the quotation below is taken.

And the third angel sounded, and there fell a great star from heaven, burning as it were a lamp, and it fell upon the third part of the rivers, and upon the fountains of waters:

And the name of the star is called Wormwood: and the third part of the waters became wormwood: and many men died of the waters, because they were made bitter.

REVELATION, ch. 8, vv. 10–11

Wormwood

This 'robust and stately plant' (Nicholas Culpeper) with its large leaves and shining golden flowers deserves a place in any garden, although it is strictly a wild flower. Its botanical name, *Inula helenium*, is in itself a clue to the legend about the plant's origin. Quoted by Pliny, it tells us that Elecampane sprang from the tears of Helen of Troy when she was carried off by Paris. In another version, it seems that she was gathering a bunch of it when he took her away. Another name for it is elfwort – and some writers claim that elves live under the plant.

Elecampane is not used in cooking, but there are references to it being grown for other purposes in the oldest herb gardens for which written records survive. The roots were candied and used as a sweetmeat, and it was said to heal wounds. There have even been claims that elecampane confers immortality.

Thomas Green, in his *Universal Herbal* of 1820, notes some of its other uses: 'the decoction is sometimes given to children for the worms, but we know not with what success: bruised and macerated in urine, with balls of ashes and whortle berries, it dyes a blue colour: the decoction of it cures sheep that have the scab; hence in some countries it is called Scab-wort, and in others Horse-heal, from its reputed virtues in curing the cutaneous diseases of horses.'

Keen flower-arrangers should try to find some elecampane, for it makes a beautiful addition to any vase of mixed flowers.

Elecampane

This delightfully scented herb has many other names, among them 'old man', 'boy's love', 'maiden's ruin' and 'garde-robe'. The seventeenth-century herbalist Nicholas Culpeper claimed that 'boiled with barleymeal, it removes pimples and wheals from the face or other parts of the body. . . . The ashes mingled with old salad oil, helps those that are bald, causing the hair to grow again.' It is not used in cooking, but may be hung up in the wardrobe among clothes (hence its name 'garde-robe') as an effective moth-repellent.

I'll give to him,
Who gathers me, more sweetness than he'd dream
Without me – more than any lily could.
I that am flowerless, being Southernwood.
  Shall I give you honesty,
  Or lad's love to wear?
  Or a wreath less fair to see,
  Juniper or Rosemary?
  Flaxenhair

Rosemary, lest you forget,
What was lief and fair,
Lad's love, sweet thro' fear and fret,
Lad's love, green and living yet,
  Flaxenhair

FINNISH BRIDE SONG

Southernwood

Mint is said to have acquired its name from a nymph of Cocytus named Minthé. She was loved by the god Hades, or Pluto, whose jealous wife Persephone turned her into a plant, in which form she has remained to this day. As mint signifies virtue in the language of flowers, perhaps the metamorphosis was a means of deliverance from a god's unwelcome attentions.

Mint was highly regarded by the Greeks and Romans as a general tonic, and it was also used to perfume bath water. The Romans brought it, together with many other herbs, to Britain with them. Virgil says that wounded deer sought out mint to heal themselves when they had been hunted and, according to Ovid, it was much used in love potions. In the Middle Ages it was used as a strewing herb to keep rooms fresh and to discourage mice, which are said not to like it.

Mint is mentioned in the Bible as one of the tithes paid by the Pharisees, in *Matthew,* chapter 23: 'Woe unto you, scribes and Pharisees, hypocrites! For ye pay tithe of mint and anise and cummin and have omitted the weightier matters of the law, judgement, mercy and faith: these ought ye to have done, and not leave the other undone.'

There are many varieties of mint. The most commonly grown is spearmint, *Mentha viridis*, widely used in cooking. Peppermint, or *Mentha piperita* is mentioned in thirteenth-century Icelandic herbals. Other kinds include apple, eau-de-cologne, pineapple and pennyroyal. Nicholas Culpeper, who mentions over thirty complaints which mint can alleviate, gives this advice:

> Applied with salt, it helps the bites of mad dogs . . . and is good to wash the heads of young children with, against all manner of breakings out, sores or scabs, and heals the chops in the fundament . . . The juice taken in vinegar, stays bleeding, stirs up venery or bodily lust. The decoction gargled in the mouth, cures the mouth and gums that are sore, and amends an ill-favoured breath.

Mint

Not all herbs have a good 'image'. Hemlock is a highly poisonous umbellifer, distinguished by an unpleasant smell. Unfortunately it is similar to both chervil and fennel and great care must be taken not to confuse it with the harmless members of the same botanical family. Everyone knows that Socrates, the philosopher, died after drinking an infusion of hemlock: it was commonly used in Ancient Greece for committing suicide. Hemlock is one of the dreaded 'witch herbs', the other two being henbane and hemp, and all three plants contain very powerful narcotic drugs. It was an ingredient of witches' incense (for which recipes still exist), used for conjuring up demons by inducing a state of trance.

Between the time of the wind and the snow,
All loathliest weeds begin to grow,
Whose coarse leaves were splashed with many a speck,
Like the water-snake's belly and the toad's back.

And thistles and nettles, and darnels rank,
And the dock, and the henbane, and hemlock dank,
Stretched out its long and hollow shank,
And stifled the air till the dead wind stank.

And plants, at whose names the verse feels loath,
Filled the place with a monstrous undergrowth,
Prickly, and pulpous and blistering, and blue,
Livid and starred with a lurid dew.

P. B. SHELLEY: 'THE SENSITIVE PLANT'

Hemlock

Parsley was used by the ancient Greeks in victors' crowns, and also in funeral rites (it was dedicated to Persephone, queen of the dead). In fact, there is a Greek saying 'He has need now of nothing but a little parsley' – that is, he is dead! It was traditionally used by the Greeks to deck tombs, as it stays green for a long time. Its meaning in the language of flowers – 'festivity' – obviously has a wide interpretation.

Parsley takes a long time to germinate, and tradition says that it has to go to the Devil and back seven times before it will sprout. There are various stories about parsley. One old wives' tale is that it will only flourish for families where the wife 'wears the trousers'. Another says that it grows for the wicked but not for the good (which is a consoling factor for those who have no success in growing it). It is supposed to be unlucky to transplant it.

Some old herbals recommend growing parsley as a crop for sheep, to prevent them getting foot rot, and Homer says that chariot horses were fed with parsley – presumably because it symbolizes strength. It is not good for small birds, however.

Parsley has a long-established role in the kitchen, both as an ingredient in sauces, stuffings, egg and savoury dishes and as an essential element in bouquets garnis. It also makes an attractive garnish.

Parsley tea (made by pouring boiling water over the leaves, allowing the mixture to infuse for twenty minutes, then straining) is said to improve the complexion and act as a tonic, but should not be drunk by anyone suffering from inflamed kidneys. Nicholas Culpeper says that 'the leaves laid to the eyes inflamed with heat or swollen, helps them . . . the juice dropped into the ears with a little wine, eases the pain.'

Parsley

Aromatic basil, either fresh or dried, is an indispensable herb in the kitchen, especially for tomato dishes. There are many stories associated with it, and those who have read the poems of Keats will know the story of poor Isabella who buried her murdered lover's head in a pot of basil and watered the plant with her tears. In India basil is regarded as the protector of the poor; in Greece it signifies hatred; but in Italy, it means love.

Madonna, wherefore has thou sent to me
  Sweet basil and mignonette?
Embleming love and health, which never yet
In the same wreath might be.
  Alas, and they are wet!
Is it with thy kisses or thy tears?
  For never rain or dew
  Such fragrance drew
From plant or flower – the very doubt endears
  My sadness ever new,
The sighs I breathe, the tears I shed for thee.

P. B. SHELLEY: 'TO EMILIA VIVIANI'

Basil

Rue was once known as 'herb of grace', for it was a symbol of repentance and sprigs of it were used to sprinkle holy water at mass. Traditionally it was thought to ward off the evil eye and also to be able to grant the gift of second sight.

I walked alone and thinking,
   And faint the nightwind blew
And stirred on mounds at crossways
   The flowers of sinner's rue.

Where the roads part they bury
   Him that his own hand slays,
And so the weed of sorrow
   Springs at the four cross ways.

By night I plucked it hueless,
   When morning broke 'twas blue:
Blue at my breast I fastened
   The flower of sinner's rue.

It seemed a herb of healing,
   A balsam and a sign,
Flower of a heart whose trouble
   Must have been worse than mine.

Dead clay that did me kindness,
   I can do none to you,
But only wear for breastknot
   The flower of sinner's rue.

A. E. HOUSMAN: 'SINNER'S RUE'

Rue

Angelica is an imposing and handsome plant, and can reach a height of 7 feet (over 2 metres), given good conditions. One story has it that its marvellous powers were revealed to a monk during a plague, and that is how it got its name. Angelica is another herb which is said to be powerful against witches. Medicinally it was used to cure digestive ailments. Today, it is a common flavouring for bitters, gin, vermouth and Chartreuse, and the candied stems are of course very popular for cake decoration.

To write a description of that which is so well known to be growing almost in every garden, I suppose is altogether needless; yet for its virtues it is of admirable use. . . . Some call this an herb of the Holy Ghost; others more moderate called it Angelica, because of its angelical virtues, and that name it retains still. . . . It is an herb of the sun in Leo; let it be gathered when he is there, the Moon applying to his good aspect. . . . It resists poison by defending and comforting the heart, blood and spirits; it doth the like against the plague and all epidemical diseases. . . . The stalks or roots candied and eaten fasting, are good preservatives in time of infection.

NICHOLAS CULPEPER: COMPLETE HERBAL

Angelica

This very fragrant herb originated in North America. It was brought to Western Europe in the seventeenth century. Another name for it is Oswego tea, after the Indian tribe of that name who made it into a drink. It is also known as bee balm, for its fragrant red flowers are very attractive to bees. The leaves may be used (sparingly) in salads or fruit cups.

Speak not – whisper not;
Here bloweth thyme and bergamot;
Softly on the evening hour,
Secret herbs their spices shower.
Dark-spiked rosemary and myrrh,
Lean-stalked, purple lavender;
Hides within her bosom, too,
All her sorrows, bitter rue

WALTER DE LA MARE: 'THE SUNKEN GARDEN' (EXTRACT)

Bergamot

Although ivy is poisonous if eaten, it was used by herbalists to soothe muscular aches and pains. To use it, wash and chop a few handfuls of ivy leaves and steep in warm vegetable oil by the fire or in the airing cupboard for a few weeks, stirring daily. Strain the oil and bottle it, and use as a rub on the aching muscles. Many traditional sayings and charms are associated with ivy – for instance, it is said that if you have more ivy than holly in your Christmas decorations you are in for bad luck during the next year. The plant is sacred to Bacchus, god of wine, and it is the symbol of faithfulness.

Shaving this morning, I look out of the window
In expectation: will another small
Tendril of ivy, dry and straw-yellow,
Have put its thin clasp on the garden wall?

O dear no. A few arid strands, a few
Curled-up leaves, are all that's left of it.
The children pulled it up for something to do.
My mouth sets in its usual post-box slit.

Fled is that vision of a bottle-green
Fur-coat of foliage muffling the pale brick,
Stamping into the flat suburban scene
A proof of beauty, lovable exotic.

KINGSLEY AMIS: 'CREEPER'

Ivy

Through the centuries the nettle has been a most useful herb to man. The young leaves can be eaten either as a green vegetable or made into soup or beer. The Romans, who introduced it into Britain, used it to sting themselves and thereby promote good circulation, while the Scandinavians wove the tough stalk fibres into fabric. Medicinally it was used by herbalists to treat rheumatism and inflammations of the skin.

Tall nettles cover up, as they have done
These many springs, the rusty harrow, the plough
Long worn out, and the roller made of stone:
Only the elm butt tops the nettles now.

This corner of the farmyard I like most:
As well as any bloom upon a flower
I like the dust on the nettles, never lost
Except to prove the sweetness of a shower.

EDWARD THOMAS: 'TALL NETTLES'

Nettle

This pretty plant has enjoyed a high reputation for both the medical treatment of human beings and for reviving any sickly plants growing near it. Its lovely Saxon name was 'maythen'. Infused in water, it makes a refreshing tea which is said to be good for women's complaints, and it lightens and brightens fair hair when used as a rinse. Planted between paving slabs or as small lawns, it is highly aromatic when walked on.

As well as their flower garden, the women cultivated a herb corner, stocked with thyme and parsley and sage for cooking, rosemary to flavour the home-made lard, lavender to scent the best clothes and peppermint, pennyroyal, horehound, camomile, tansy, balm, and rue for physic. They made a good deal of camomile tea, which they drank freely to ward off colds, to soothe the nerves, and as a general tonic. A large jug of this was always prepared and stood ready for heating up after confinements. The horehound was used with honey in a preparation to be taken for sore throats and colds on the chest.

FLORA THOMPSON: LARK RISE TO CANDLEFORD

Camomile

Acknowledgements

The author and publishers are grateful for permission to quote copyright passages from the following books: extract from *Puck of Pook's Hill* by Rudyard Kipling reprinted by permission of A. P. Watt Ltd; extract from *Provence* by Ford Madox Ford reprinted by permission of George Allen & Unwin; extracts from *Lark Rise to Candleford* by Flora Thompson (1954) reprinted by permission of Oxford University Press; extract from 'Creeper' from *A Case of Samples* by Kingsley Amis reprinted by permission of Victor Gollancz Ltd and A. D. Peters & Co. Ltd; the Literary Trustees of Walter de la Mare and the Society of Authors as their representative for extracts from 'The Hawthorn Hath a Deadly Smell' and 'The Sunken Garden'; the Society of Authors as the literary representative of the Estate of A. E. Housman and Jonathan Cape Ltd, publisher of A. E. Housman's *Collected Poems*; extract from *The Go-Between* by L. P. Hartley reprinted by permission of Hamish Hamilton Ltd.

Hutchinson & Co. (Publishers) Ltd
An imprint of the Hutchinson Publishing Group
3 Fitzroy Square, London W1P 6JD
Hutchinson Group (Australia) Pty Ltd
30–32 Cremorne Street, Richmond South, Victoria 3121
PO Box 151, Broadway, New South Wales 2007
Hutchinson Group (NZ) Ltd
32–34 View Road, PO Box 40-086, Glenfield, Auckland 10
Hutchinson Group (SA) Pty Ltd
PO Box 337, Bergvlei 2012, South Africa
First published 1980
Designed and produced for Hutchinson & Co. by
BELLEW & HIGTON
Bellew & Higton Publishers Ltd
19–21 Conway Street London W1P 6JD

ISBN 0 09 143170 0
Printed and bound in Spain

by Printer Industria Gráfica S.A.
Provenza, 388/Barcelona, San Vicente dels Horts 1980
Depósito Legal B. 16014 – 1980